Designed to DELIGHT

Activities to Enhance Children's Enjoyment of Books

Preschool-Grade 3 · by Doris Bullock

Fearon Teacher Aids
a division of
David S. Lake Publishers
Belmont, California

Publisher: Mel Cebulash
Editorial director: Ina Tabibian
Editor: Emily Hutchinson
Managing editor: Susan J. Riddle
Production editor: Stephen Feinstein
Design director: Eleanor Mennick
Designer: Colleen Forbes
Illustrator: Duane Bibby
Manufacturing director: Casimira Kostecki

ISBN-0-8224-2255-7

Library of Congress Catalog Card Number: 85-50491

Printed in the United States of America

1. 9 8 7 6 5 4 3 2

Table of Contents

Introduction

Designed to Delight is a collection of many tried and tested activities that correlate with the story-telling session. It is intended for use by teachers, librarians, and library media specialists who are looking for methods to increase the pleasure children derive from books.

The activities in this book were used not only to enrich the students' knowledge of various books and authors but also to help develop and strengthen skills in visual discrimination, eye-hand coordination, oral expression, and fine motor control. Each page follows the same format: a brief summary of a children's book, bibliographical information about the book, a description of the activity recommended to add to children's enjoyment of the book, and the procedure for the activity. Some projects require the use of a reproducible activity page or pages, which have been included.

Tips for Reading Aloud

■ Choose a book that you enjoy. This is very important. Your enthusiasm and pleasure will be contagious.

■ Before the story session, practice reading the story aloud until you are very familiar with it.

■ Consider how you will share the book. Will you stand, sit on a chair, sit on the floor, or sit on a low stool? Many authorities agree that sitting on a low stool is the best position for reading to a group of young children. This places you just above the heads of the children and lets everyone see the pictures if, as is most likely, the children are sitting on the floor.

■ Have students sit in such an arrangement that everyone can see and hear clearly.

■ Before you read the book, state the title and the author's name.

■ Keep an eye on your audience as you read.

■ Introduce the book by discussing something relevant to its content or by referring to something the students have been studying. After reading the story, discuss it and get the students' reaction to it.

Suggestions for Implementing Activities

■ You should be familiar with the interests, needs, and abilities of the students you are working with.

■ In most cases, the book should be shared with the students before they do the related activity. Reading aloud, using the flannel board, showing filmstrips, or using other media will provide variety and enhance book presentations. When it is appropriate, you might consider wearing a costume or using other props to stimulate and sustain student interest.

■ Preplanning is essential to having a successful activity. Make sure that enough materials are available for all participants. Some activities involving cutting and pasting may require additional time. Plan ahead for adjustments in your schedule; modify activities to suit your needs.

■ Many items recommended for the activities may be brought in by students or borrowed from colleagues. Others may be purchased at nominal prices.

Always Room for One More

This is an old Scottish folksong about a couple and their ten children. They share their home with whoever comes by on a stormy day, saying "Always room for one more!" But is there? The results are disastrous for a while, but everything turns out better than before. (This verse should be read with a wee bit of a lilt.)

Nic Leodhas, Sorche. New York: Holt, Rinehart and Winston, 1965.

32 pages, illustrated, K–grade 3

 ACTIVITY: Make pictures for a door or bulletin board.

Materials

Drawing paper, cut to desired picture size

Crayons or colored pencils

Plastic or cutout paper letters to spell title

Thumbtacks or tape

Door or bulletin board

Procedure

Give each student a piece of paper. Have the students draw pictures of themselves. Display the completed pictures on a door or bulletin board. Add the title, "Always Room for One More."

Note: Because the picture display conveys such a warm message, it is especially effective at media centers. It is also a good display to use for Children's Book Week.

The Amazing Bone

Pearl, the pig, is dawdling on the way home from school. While she is enjoying the beauty of the forest, something or someone starts talking to her. It's a talking bone! She picks it up to take home with her so that she can amaze her parents. Then she runs into trouble. Some highway robbers want her pocketbook, but the amazing bone comes to her rescue. Next, Pearl meets a fox who is determined to have her for dinner. With some difficulty and a little bit of magic, the bone saves her again.

Steig, William. New York: Farrar, Straus, Giroux, 1976. 32 pages, illustrated, preschool–grade 3

 ACTIVITY: Tell a story with props.

Materials

Large bone

Pocketbook

Procedure

Before the story session, put the bone inside the pocketbook. At the beginning of the session, tell the students that something amazing is in the pocketbook. Allow them to make a few guesses about what it is.

Before you read the story, have one student open the pocketbook and show the bone to the other students. Inform them that the bone is going to play an important role in saving a pig's life.

Read the story aloud to the students.

Ben's Trumpet

Ben enjoys listening to the jazz being played at the nearby Zig Zag Jazz Club. Most of all, he likes the sound of the trumpet. At home and on his block, Ben pretends to play an imaginary trumpet. His friends laugh at him and make him feel sad. One day, the trumpeter from the club invites him to play a real trumpet.

Isadora, Rachel. New York: Greenwillow Books, 1979.
32 pages, illustrated, K–grade 3

ACTIVITY: Listen to the sounds of a trumpet.

Materials

Trumpet

Picture of Louis Armstrong or Dizzy Gillespie

Recording by Armstrong or Gillespie

Record player

Procedure

Show the trumpet to the students. Play it or have someone else do so.

Have students pretend they are playing the trumpet, as Ben did in the story.

Show the picture of Louis Armstrong or Dizzy Gillespie. Tell students about the musician and play some of his music.

The Best Valentine in the World

Ferdinand Fox starts in plenty of time (on November 5, to be exact) to make a special valentine for Florette Fox. When he learns that she has forgotten Valentine's Day, Ferdinand is disappointed, but not for long.

Sharmat, Marjorie Weinman. New York: Holiday House, 1982. 32 pages, illustrated, K–grade 3

 ACTIVITY: Design a valentine.

Materials

Valentines, precut from red or pink construction paper

Box of items from outdoors—seeds, pieces of bark, twigs, and the like

Assortment of scraps—buttons, lace, ribbons, yarn, paper doilies, and such

Felt-tip markers

Glue

Procedure

Give a precut valentine to each student. Have students choose various decorative items to glue onto their valentines. Have them use felt-tip markers to write messages on their valentines.

Have students display their valentines on a table or bulletin board, exchange them, or take them home.

The Big Dipper

This informational book tells young readers how to locate the Big Dipper and the Little Dipper, and explains how to use them for finding directions. It also gives facts and legends about these two constellations.

Branley, Franklyn M. New York: Thomas Y. Crowell, 1962. 40 pages, illustrated, K–grade 2

 ACTIVITY: Form the shape of the Big Dipper.

Materials

Black construction paper

Pencils

Pieces of Styrofoam™

Glue

Procedure

Give students black construction paper and pencils. Have them draw dots to represent the Big Dipper, as shown in the illustration. Have students put a dab of glue over each dot and put a piece of Styrofoam™ on each dab of glue.

If time permits, follow the same procedure for the Little Dipper and other constellations.

The Blind Men and the Elephant

This is a retelling of an old fable from India. Six blind men travel to the palace of the Rajah to find out what an elephant is like. They argue about the animal because each blind man touches only one part of it.

Quigley, Lillian. New York: Charles Scribner's Sons, 1959. 32 pages, illustrated, K–grade 3

 ACTIVITY: Identify hidden objects through touch.

Materials

Bag

Variety of items—fruits, vegetables, school supplies, small toys, and the like

Procedure

Without allowing students to see the item, place one thing inside the bag. Have each student put a hand inside the bag and feel the item. Then ask each child to describe how the item feels.

Write the students' descriptions on the chalkboard or on a large piece of paper. Have students use clues from the descriptions to identify the hidden item. Refer to the story, noting how the blind men realized that they had to put all the parts together.

After students name the item, remove it from the bag and show it to them. Follow the same procedure with the other items.

Crictor

When Madame Louise Bodot receives an O-shaped package in the mail and finds out that it is a boa constrictor sent by her son, she screams. Wouldn't you? But Crictor is an affectionate boa constrictor and a good pet. When he attends classes that Madame Bodot teaches, he learns to form letters and numbers with his body. He makes a good playmate for the children. Then he does something that earns him a medal and a statue in his honor. What a snake!

Ungerer, Tomi. New York: Harper and Row, 1958.
32 pages, illustrated, preschool–grade 3

 ACTIVITY: Form letters and numbers with clay.

Materials

Clay
Cardboard

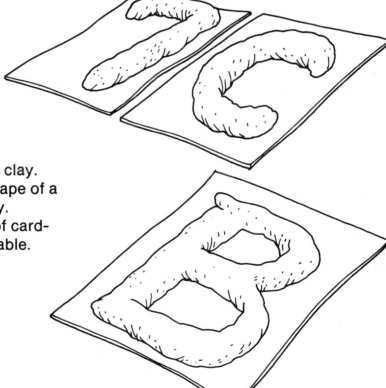

Procedure

Give each student a piece of clay. Have each student form the shape of a letter or a number with the clay.

Place the shape on a piece of cardboard. Display the work on a table.

The Easter Egg Artists

The artistic Abbots, a family of rabbits, design and decorate Easter eggs from January to Easter. From October to January, they go south on vacation. This year they decorate their car, other people's houses, and even bridges and airplanes. When they get home, Orson, the son, helps with the Easter eggs. He invents comic Easter eggs—a big success—and soon goes on to decorating flagpoles.

Adams, Adrienne. New York: Charles Scribner's Sons, 1976. 32 pages, illustrated, K–grade 3

 ACTIVITY: Design comic Easter eggs.

Materials

Precut paper eggs in various sizes and colors

Assortment of scraps—buttons, cotton, yarn, and the like

Crayons or felt-tip markers

Glue

Scissors

Plastic or cutout paper letters to spell title

Thumbtacks

Bulletin board

Procedure

Give each student several paper eggs. Have the students use scraps, glue, and crayons or markers to decorate their eggs in a humorous way.

Display the finished eggs on a bulletin board. Add a title, such as "The Comic Egg Parade."

Flat Stanley

Stanley Lambchop is flattened by a falling bulletin board one night. Being four feet tall, about a foot wide, and half an inch thick has lots of advantages. Stanley can travel through the mail, for example, and his dad can roll him up like a parcel and carry him. He can be a kite, too. But what good can he do? Can he be helpful in society? Stanley has an idea. . . .

Brown, Jeff. New York: Harper and Row, 1964.
48 pages, illustrated, grades 1–3

 ACTIVITY: Make a "Flat Stanley."

Materials

Felt squares

Scissors

Glue

Plastic or cutout paper letters to spell title

Felt-tip markers

Construction paper

Thumbtacks

Bulletin board

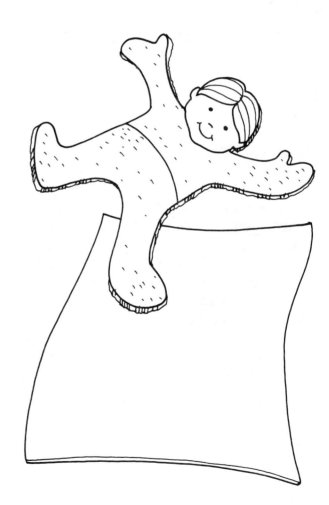

Procedure

Give each student a felt square. Have each student use a marker to draw a picture of Stanley on the felt. Then have the children cut out the felt shapes and glue them to the construction paper.

Tack the mounted cutouts to a bulletin board. Add the title, "Flat Stanley."

Goggles!

Peter and Archie find motorcycle goggles in an old neighborhood dump. They are having fun with the goggles, but they soon run into trouble. Some bullies want the goggles and start a fight, but Peter, Archie, and Peter's dog Willie outsmart them.

Keats, Ezra Jack. New York: Macmillan, 1969.
32 pages, illustrated, K–grade 3

 ACTIVITY: Make a pair of goggles.

Materials

Plastic holders (from six-packs of soda)

Pipe cleaners

Scissors

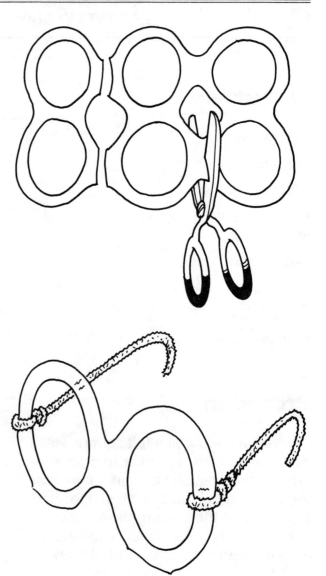

Procedure

Cut each plastic holder in thirds, so that you have three pairs of circles.

Give each student one pair of circles and two pipe cleaners. Have students attach a pipe cleaner to each side of the pair of circles. Have them wind one end of each pipe cleaner around the plastic a few times so it will stay in place. Have them bend the other end of each pipe cleaner so the goggles will fit around their ears. Allow students to wear their goggles for a while.

Greg's Microscope

Greg asks his dad for a microscope after seeing his friend Billy's. Then Greg, his dad, his mom, Mrs. Broom, and Billy all learn many interesting things—about salt, sugar, pepper, hair, thread, one-celled animals, and more.

Selsam, Millicent Ellis. New York: Harper and Row, 1963.
64 pages, illustrated, K–grade 3

 ACTIVITY: Observe items under a microscope.

Materials

Microscope and slides

Cotton thread

Strand of hair

Dash of salt

Dash of sugar

Dash of pepper

Water

Procedure

Before the story session, prepare some slides using the salt mixed with a drop of water. Prepare other slides, some using sugar mixed with a drop of water and some using pepper mixed with a drop of water. Allow slides to dry. Set them aside.

Read the story aloud to the students. After the story session, place thread and hair, one at a time, under the microscope. Have students look through the microscope and describe what each specimen looks like. Then, have them look at the salt, sugar, and pepper slides. Ask them to compare the dried slides with the slides of thread and hair.

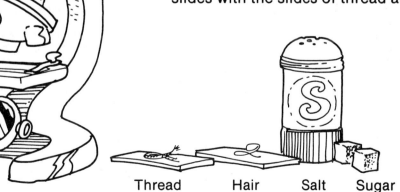

Thread　　Hair　　Salt　　Sugar

The Grouchy Ladybug

A grouchy ladybug spots a leaf with many aphids on it. Not wanting to share, the grouchy ladybug challenges a friendly ladybug to fight. The grouchy ladybug moves on and continues to pick fights with other animals. The animals she fights with keep getting larger and larger. Finally she meets a blue whale!
   Carle, Eric. New York: Harper and Row, 1977.
   44 pages, illustrated, preschool–grade 2

 ACTIVITY: Dramatize a story.

Materials

Paper plates

Felt-tip markers

Popsicle sticks

Glue

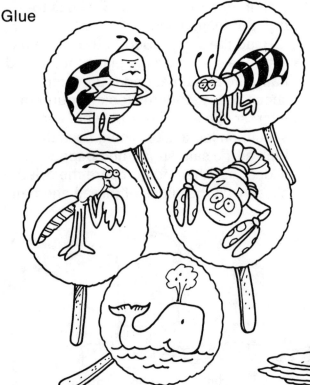

Procedure

On paper plates, draw and color these characters, one per plate:

Friendly Ladybug	Lobster
Grouchy Ladybug	Skunk
Boa Constrictor	Leaf
Yellow Jacket	Hyena
Stag Beetle	Gorilla
Praying Mantis	Rhinoceros
Sparrow	Whale

Glue a popsicle stick to the back of each paper plate. Give one plate to each student. Have students act out the story, each one playing the character shown on his or her plate. Have them hold up the plates as they act out the story.

Hailstones and Halibut Bones

Twelve poems discuss what a color is. Red, purple, gold, black, brown, blue, gray, orange, pink, green, yellow, and white are the colors featured.

O'Neill, Mary. New York: Doubleday, 1961.
64 pages, illustrated, K–grade 2

 ACTIVITY: Have a festival of colors.

Materials

Magazines

Poster paper

Paste

Scissors

Procedure

About a week before you plan to read the book aloud, divide the class into small groups. Assign a different color to each group. Have students look through magazines and cut out pictures of items that are the designated color or are primarily that color. Then have the members of each group get together and paste their pictures on a piece of poster paper, creating a collage.

During your story session, display each poster separately. Have students name things that are the same color as the items in the poster. Then read the poem.

Continue this activity until all the posters have been displayed and all the colors have been discussed.

Harold and the Purple Crayon

One night, Harold decides to go for a walk in the moonlight. It's a good thing he's brought his purple crayon because he has to draw a moon. Then he has to draw a path and a forest and all sorts of things. It's lucky for him that he remembers where his bedroom window is because it is soon time to be going to sleep. When the moon's out, his window is always around it, so that's where he draws his window. Now he can get back home.

Johnson, Crockett. New York: Harper and Row, 1981.
64 pages, illustrated, preschool–grade 3

ACTIVITY: Draw a scene with purple crayons.

Materials

Purple crayons

White shelf paper, cut to desired size

Thumbtacks or tape

Bulletin board or wall

Procedure

Spread the white paper on a long table or on the floor. Print "The Purple Crayon" in large letters at the top of the paper. Have each student use a purple crayon to draw one or two things on the paper.

Display the finished work on a bulletin board or on a wall.

Harriet Reads Signs and More Signs

Harriet, the elephant, goes to visit her grandmother. Along the way she reads all the signs she sees. "To Town," "Don't Walk," "Walk," "Stop," and "Keep Off the Grass" are just a few of them. Her favorite sign of all is "Grandma's House."
Maestro, Betsy, and Giulio Maestro. New York: Crown, 1981. 32 pages, illustrated, K–grade 3

 ACTIVITY: Create picture scenes with signs.

Materials

Drawing paper

Crayons

Copies of the signs on pages 16 and 17

Scissors

Paste

Thumbtacks or tape

Bulletin board or wall

Procedure

Distribute the copies of signs to the students. Have each student select a sign or signs to use as part of a picture. Have each student paste the sign or signs on drawing paper, do an illustration around them, and color the entire picture.

Display the illustrations on a bulletin board or on a wall.

DON'T WALK

SCHOOL

LIBRARY

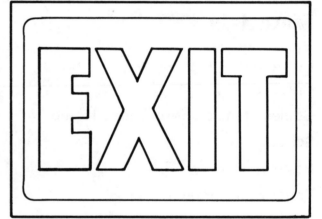

SCHOOL CROSSING

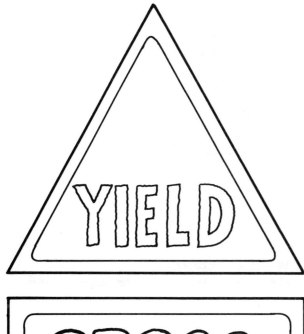

Heavy Is a Hippopotamus

What is "heavy"? What does that mean? A log is not heavy to an elephant; a crumb is heavy to an ant. The concept of weight is explained in this book. Weight has nothing to do with shape, size, or color; it has to do only with the heaviness or lightness of a thing. This book also introduces students to the concepts of ounce, pound, and ton.

Schlein, Miriam. New York: William R. Scott, 1954.
40 pages, illustrated, K–grade 3

 ACTIVITY: Lift and weigh objects.

Materials

Two bags (same size)

Two boxes (different sizes)

Various objects

Scale

Procedure

Fill one bag with heavy objects; fill the other bag with light objects. Fill the smaller box with heavy objects; fill the larger box with light objects.

Allow students to guess which of the two bags is heavier. Have them lift the bags and compare the weights. Put each bag on the scale and note the difference. Repeat this procedure with the boxes.

Explain to students that the size of an object does not necessarily determine its weight.

If You Take a Pencil

"If you take a pencil, you can draw two cats" and many other things. This counting book leads the reader to all kinds of treasures that can be created with a pencil. It describes how a pencil may be used to draw cats, birds, fingers, orange trees, and other objects in quantities from two to twelve.

Testa, Fulvio. New York: Dial Press, 1982.
28 pages, illustrated, preschool–grade 2

 ACTIVITY: Create a treasure with a pencil.

Materials

Box

Pencils

Paper

Thumbtacks

Plastic or cutout paper letters to spell title

Bulletin board

Procedure

Before the story session, place pencils and paper inside the box. Read the story aloud to the students.

After the story session, make a ceremony of opening the box to find the treasure inside. Then pass out paper and pencils to the students. Have them create their own treasures, as suggested by the story.

Display drawings on a bulletin board. Add the title, "If You Take a Pencil."

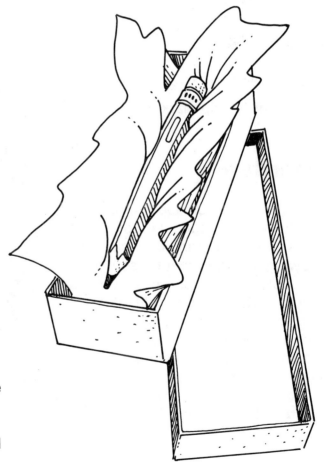

The Important Book

In everything there is something of importance. "The important thing about a spoon is that you eat with it." "The important thing about rain is that it is wet." "The important thing about glass is that you see through it." There is much to say about daisies, grass, snow, wind, and other things. But everything has at least one reason it is important.

Brown, Margaret Wise. New York: Harper and Row, 1949. 24 pages, illustrated, preschool–grade 1

 ACTIVITY: Identify and draw things of importance.

Materials

Drawing paper

Crayons or felt-tip markers

Procedure

Lead a discussion about what is important to the students. Some of the topics you might bring up include the following: an important person, toy, food, pet, game, book, season, holiday, place, television show, date, idea, song, movie.

After students have thought about what is important to them and why, distribute drawing paper and crayons or felt-tip markers. Have students draw pictures of what is important.

The Jelly Bean Contest

A group of boys eager to win a new football try to guess the
number of jelly beans in a jar.
Darling, Kathy. Champaign, Illinois: Garrard, 1972.
64 pages, illustrated, K–grade 3

 ACTIVITY: Guess the number of jelly beans in the jar.

Materials

Jar with lid

Jelly beans

Shoe box with lid

Procedure

Fill a jar with jelly beans, counting
them as you do it. Place the jar in a
prominent place.

Cut a slit in the lid of the shoe box;
place the shoe box next to the jar of
jelly beans.

Have students guess the number of
jelly beans in the jar. Allow each student one guess. Have them write their
guesses on paper and put them in the
shoe box. (Remind students to put their
names on their papers!)

Offer a prize (such as a paperback
book) for the person whose guess
comes closest.

Note: A good time for this contest is
during Book Week or National Library
Week.

Journey Cake, Ho!

When times are tough at Johnny's farm and the food supply is low, his folks send him away. The Journey Cake in Johnny's sack jumps out and rolls away. It leads many animals to the barnyard of Johnny's home, making the folks and Johnny happy again.

Sawyer, Ruth. New York: Viking, 1953.
52 pages, illustrated, K–grade 3

 ACTIVITY: Make a journey cake.

Materials

Clay
Frying pan

Procedure

Give each student a piece of clay. Have each child roll the clay and flatten it so it looks like a pancake.

When the students have finished making their "pancakes," give each one an opportunity to put the pancake in the frying pan and pretend to cook it.

Katy No-Pocket

Katy Kangaroo is distressed because she has no pocket in which to carry Freddy, her baby. Her friend, Mrs. Crocodile, says that she carries Catherine on her back, but that doesn't work for Katy and Freddy. Mrs. Monkey carries Jocko in her arms, but Katy's arms are too short. None of the other animals help. Finally, a carpenter who has an apron helps to solve Katy's problem.

Payne, Emmy. Boston: Houghton Mifflin, 1973.
32 pages, illustrated, K–grade 3

 ACTIVITY: Fill Katy's pockets.

Materials

Posterboard

Felt-tip markers

#10 envelopes

Paste

Scissors

Drawing paper, cut to 3½" × 5"

Procedure

Using felt-tip markers, draw a large picture of Katy on the posterboard. (You may project and trace the picture on this page.)

Seal the envelopes and cut them in thirds. Discard the middle thirds. Paste the sides with the flaps to the front of Katy, arranging the envelope pieces as if they are pockets in her apron. Draw details (apron string and other decorations) so it looks as if Katy is wearing an apron.

Display Katy on an easel or a chair.

Distribute drawing paper and markers to students. Have them place the paper vertically on their desks and draw an animal or a favorite treasure on it. Tell them to draw most of the picture near the top of the paper so it will show when the paper is put in Katy's pocket. When they are finished, have the students, in turn, put their pictures in Katy's pockets.

The King's Flower

The King always wanted everything of his to be bigger and better than anyone else's. He needed a ladder to get in and out of bed, and it took two men just to carry his toothbrush. When a beautiful, but small, red tulip blooms in his huge flowerpot, the King learns that biggest does not always mean best.

Anno, Mitsumasa. New York: Collins, 1979.

32 pages, illustrated, preschool–grade 3

 ACTIVITY: Make flowers fit for a king.

Materials

Wallpaper scraps

Pencils

Bulletin board

White bulletin-board paper

Scissors

Thumbtacks

Green felt-tip markers

Plastic or cutout paper letters to spell title

Flowers Fit for a King

Procedure

Give each student a scrap of wallpaper. Have each student draw a tulip on the wallpaper and then cut it out.

Cover the bulletin board with white paper, and have the students tack their tulips to the board. Have them use green felt-tip markers to draw stems and leaves. Add the title, "Flowers Fit for a King."

A Kiss Is Round

This picture book teaches the concept of roundness, using brief verses to go along with the colorful illustrations.

Budney, Blossom. New York: Lothrop, Lee & Shepard, 1954. 32 pages, illustrated, K–grade 3

 ACTIVITY: Use round objects to introduce the concept of *round*.

Materials

Round objects—balls, coins, oranges, bracelets, rings, plates, and the like

Procedure

Display round objects on a table or a shelf. Allow students to handle them. Have the students look around the room or outside the window to find more things that are round. Have each student identify one of the round objects.

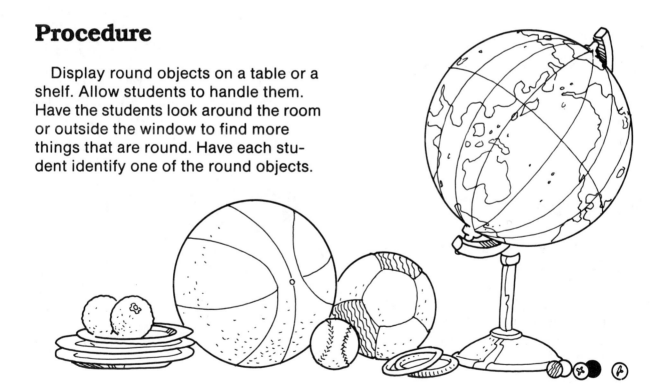

Let's Make Rabbits

The pencil and the scissors decide to make rabbits. The pencil draws a rabbit in black and white, and the scissors make one from colorful scraps of paper. The rabbits are hungry, so they ask the pencil and the scissors for food. They get two carrots—one is sketched and the other is made of pieces of cut paper. One day the rabbits discover that they are *real* rabbits.

Lionni, Leo. New York: Pantheon Books, 1982.
32 pages, illustrated, preschool–grade 2

ACTIVITY: Make rabbits.

Materials

Drawing paper

Pencils

Scraps of brightly colored paper

Paste

Cotton balls

Felt-tip markers

Procedure

Distribute materials to the students. Have each student draw a rabbit on the drawing paper. Then have the children cut or tear pieces of colored paper and paste the pieces within the outline of the rabbit's body. Show them how to paste on a cotton ball for the tail. Have them use felt-tip markers to draw in eyes, whiskers, and other details.

Little Blue and Little Yellow

Two friends, Little Blue and Little Yellow, hug each other
"green" and go out to play. What happens when their own
parents don't recognize them?
>**Lionni, Leo.** New York: Astor-Honor, 1959.
>44 pages, illustrated, K–grade 1

 ACTIVITY: Mix blue and yellow colors.

Materials

Pieces of plastic, sheets of acetate, or plates

Food coloring (blue and yellow)

Spatulas or straws

Procedure

On a piece of plastic, a sheet of acetate, or a plate, place one drop of blue food coloring and one drop of yellow food coloring. Use a spatula to mix the drops together, or blow on them through a straw. Have students observe how the colors change to green when they are mixed.

Millions of Cats

The very old woman wants a "sweet little fluffy cat," so the very old man goes out to get one. He cannot choose just one, so he comes home with millions (and billions and trillions) of cats. How will they choose the prettiest cat?

Ga'g, Wanda. New York: Coward-McCann, 1928.
32 pages, illustrated, K–grade 3

 ACTIVITY: Make "millions" of cats.

Materials

Construction paper (assorted colors)

Scissors

Crayons

Bulletin board

Thumbtacks

Plastic or cutout paper letters to spell title

Procedure

Have each student draw a picture of a cat on construction paper and cut it out.

Have the students tack their pictures to the bulletin board.

Add the title, "Millions of Cats."

Millions of Cats

Monster Bubbles: A Counting Book

Cute monsters of all kinds blow blue and pink bubbles in amounts from one to twenty.
Nolan, Dennis. New Jersey: Prentice-Hall, 1976.
32 pages, illustrated, preschool–grade 2

 ACTIVITY: Make bubbles.

Materials

Copy of "Bubble Fun," page 30, for each student

Crayons

Bubble soap and pipes (one pipe per student)

Bowls

Procedure

Distribute the copies of "Bubble Fun" to the students. Have each student draw monster bubbles inside the giant bubble. When the children are finished, have them count the number of bubbles they have made and write the number in the blank.

Pour the bubble soap into several bowls so it's easy to use. Then give each student a bubble pipe. Let students use the bubble soap and pipes to have fun blowing and counting bubbles.

Bubble Fun

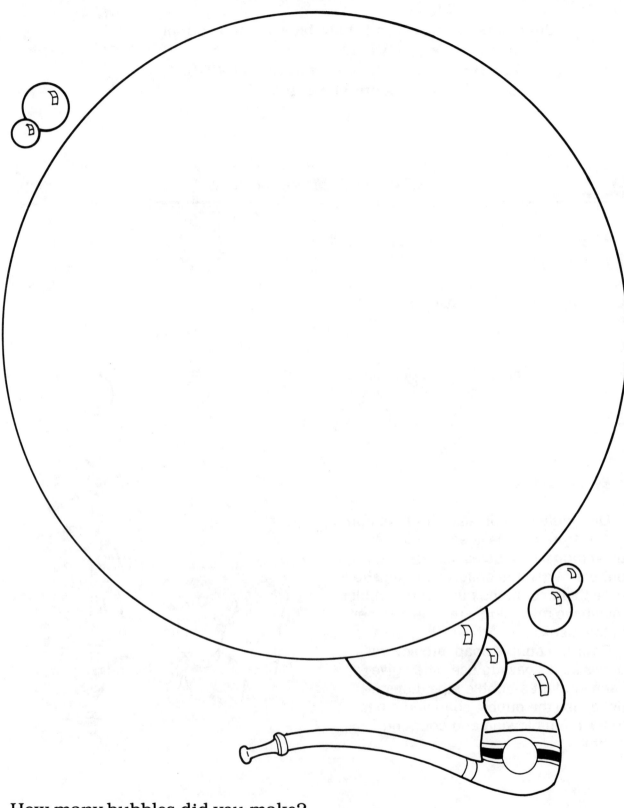

How many bubbles did you make? _____

Designed to Delight reproducible page, © 1986 David S. Lake Publishers

Mrs Pig's Bulk Buy

One day Mrs Pig decided to buy six bottles of ketchup for her ten piglets. They always wanted ketchup on everything she cooked for them. When the piglets realized that ketchup was all they would have for each meal, they learned to eat just a little of it. Ever since then, little piglets are not white but pink, so "be careful with that ketchup bottle."

Rayner, Mary. New York: Atheneum, 1981.
32 pages, illustrated, preschool–grade 2

ACTIVITY: Use props to tell a story.

Materials

Bottles of ketchup (different brands)

Procedure

Show the bottles of ketchup to the students. Have the students take turns naming the foods they put ketchup on. Ask them which is their favorite ketchup. Have them tell why.

Tell students that you are going to read a story to them about some piglets who wanted ketchup on everything.

Before you read the ending, ask the students if they think the piglets will continue to want a lot of ketchup. Ask them to give reasons for their answers.

Finish the story.

101 Dalmatians

Ten Dalmatian puppies are stolen by dog thieves. When the puppies' parents attempt to rescue them, they find a room full of Dalmatian puppies, all in need of a rescue!
  Disney, Walt. New York: Random House, 1981.
  44 pages, illustrated, K–grade 3

 ACTIVITY: Paint spots on a Dalmatian.

Materials

Copy of "Dalmatian," page 33, for each student

Black or dark brown watercolor or tempera

Paintbrushes

Procedure

  Tell students the following facts about the Dalmatian: It is named after Dalmatia, an area on the Adriatic coast of Yugoslavia, because this is where it was first found. It is a short-haired, white dog with dark brown or black spots. It is also called "English coach dog," "carriage dog," "firehouse dog," and "plum-pudding dog." When a Dalmatian is born, it is pure white; the spots appear after three or four weeks.
  Distribute a copy of "Dalmatian" to each student. Have the students paint spots on the Dalmatian.

Dalmatian

One to Ten, Count Again

From one bull in a china shop to ten mice in a store, readers count the animals hidden in the pictures.

Livermore, Elaine. Boston: Houghton Mifflin, 1973.
48 pages, illustrated, K–grade 3

ACTIVITY: Find and count the hidden animals.

Materials

Opaque projector

Screen or white wall

Pointer (ruler)

Procedure

Project the right-hand pages of the book. As you read the text, have students find the correct number of animals hidden on each page. Have students take turns pointing to the animals as they find them.

Owl and Other Scrambles

Can you make a picture of a camel, using the letters in the word *camel*? How about an airplane, a house, a reindeer, or a queen? This book has at least one word-picture for each letter of the alphabet (except *X* and *Y*). It's fun to figure out the word that's hidden in the picture.

    Weil, Lisl. New York: Dutton, 1980.

    32 pages, illustrated, preschool–grade 2

 ACTIVITY: Unscramble the picture puzzles.

Materials

Opaque projector

Screen or white wall

Pointer (ruler)

Procedure

    Project each picture in the book. As you do so, point to each letter. Have students say the letters. Encourage them to figure out what the picture puzzle spells, using the picture itself as a clue. Provide assistance if needed.

Note: *Gnome* is a bad choice for the *G* page, especially for this age level.

People

Four billion people—all different—live on our planet, and by the year 2000, there will be six billion. The differences are in everything—looks, homes, jobs, religions, holidays, pets, and more. This book reminds us how interesting all our differences are.

Spier, Peter. New York: Doubleday, 1980.
48 pages, illustrated, grades 1-3

 ACTIVITY: Discuss objects from various countries.

Materials

Various items that come from other countries—money, costumes or typical clothing, foods, books, art objects, stamps, kitchenware, and the like

Globe or world map

Index cards

Pen

Procedure

On index cards, print information about each item you have collected (country of origin, what the item is used for, what it is made of, and any other pertinent information). Display the items on a table and place the corresponding card next to each item. After the story session, discuss each item separately. Use a globe or a map to point out the country of origin for each item.

Petunia's Christmas

Petunia the goose falls in love with Charles, who is being fattened for Christmas. She has only three weeks to think of a way to save him from becoming Christmas dinner. She finally makes enough Christmas wreaths to sell, and she's able to offer a bag of coins for Charles's freedom. They marry on Christmas Day.

Duvoisin, Roger. New York: Alfred A. Knopf, 1952.
40 pages, illustrated, K–grade 3

 ACTIVITY: Make tissue-paper geese (Petunia and Charles).

Materials

Posterboard

Felt-tip marker

White tissue paper

Thumbtacks

Paste

Bulletin board

Procedure

Using a felt-tip marker, draw a picture of Charles and Petunia on the posterboard. Tack the poster to a bulletin board.

Have students tear and roll up very small pieces of tissue paper. Let them take turns pasting the pieces of tissue paper on the pictures until the geese are completely covered.

The Popcorn Book

Interesting facts about popcorn are presented in this book. While one twin brother reads about the history, varieties, and uses of popcorn, the other twin cooks some. One fact is that on a hot, dry day in the American Midwest, all the popcorn in the fields started popping. The people got out snow shovels, thinking it was a blizzard! As the first twin reads this, the other twin notices that he put too much popcorn in the pot—they have a popcorn blizzard in the kitchen! This book is an interesting mixture of science and fun.

de Paola, Tomie. New York: Holiday House, 1978.
32 pages, illustrated, K–grade 3

 ACTIVITY: Make popcorn.

Materials

Popcorn

Corn popper

Cooking oil

Large bowl

Butter and salt, if desired

Procedure

Follow the directions for your corn popper or the directions that are on the last page of *The Popcorn Book* to pop some popcorn. As students listen to the popcorn popping, tell them again what makes the kernel pop. Inform students that the states of Nebraska, Indiana, and Iowa produce most of the popcorn in the United States.

Enjoy eating the popcorn.

The Queen Who Couldn't Bake Gingerbread

This is an adaptation of a German folktale. King Pilaf and Princess Calliope were looking for certain talents in each other—the king wanted a wife who could make good gingerbread, and the princess wanted a husband who could play the slide trombone. Unfortunately, the desired talents were lacking in both of them. But they marry anyway and promise never to mention gingerbread and slide trombones again. One year later, they have a very bad day. Their argument is resolved in the best possible way.

Van Woerkom, Dorothy. New York: Alfred A. Knopf, 1975. 32 pages, illustrated, K–grade 3

 ACTIVITY: Make gingerbread.

Materials

Gingerbread mix

Baking and mixing utensils

Oven

Serving dish

Note: If an oven is not available, serve previously baked gingerbread.

Procedure

Allow students to take turns assisting you as you prepare gingerbread from a mix.

After the gingerbread has been baked and has cooled, cut it into small pieces, place the pieces on a serving dish, and serve. As you serve the gingerbread, make a ceremony out of referring to the students as "the class that could bake gingerbread."

Rain

This wordless picture book shows the adventures of a brother and sister during a rainstorm. They splash through puddles and see their reflections in them, stand under laundry on a clothesline, make footprints in the mud, see a sparkling spider's web, and do many other things. When the wind picks up, they hurry back to a cozy home, a steaming bath, a family dinner, and a quiet evening. The next morning they look out on a clean, still-wet world.

Spier, Peter. New York: Doubleday, 1982.
40 pages, illustrated, K–grade 3

 ACTIVITY: Interpret a picture story.

Materials

Book

Procedure

Have students sit in a semicircle or any other arrangement in which they can easily see the pictures. As you turn the pages, have students, in turn, tell what is happening in each picture.

After they have interpreted the picture story, have students discuss what they do when it rains.

The Red Carpet

A very important guest is expected at Hotel Bellevue. When the red carpet is rolled out, it keeps rolling and rolling.

Parkin, Rex. New York: Macmillan, 1967.

48 pages, illustrated, K–grade 3

 ACTIVITY: Make red carpets for very important people.

Materials

Red construction paper

Crayons or felt-tip pens

Procedure

Give each student a piece of red construction paper (cut to desired size). Have each child draw a fringe on each end of the construction paper to make it look like a carpet. Then ask each student to write the name of a very important person on the paper.

Allow the students to talk briefly about their important people.

Display the red carpets on a wall or on a bulletin board.

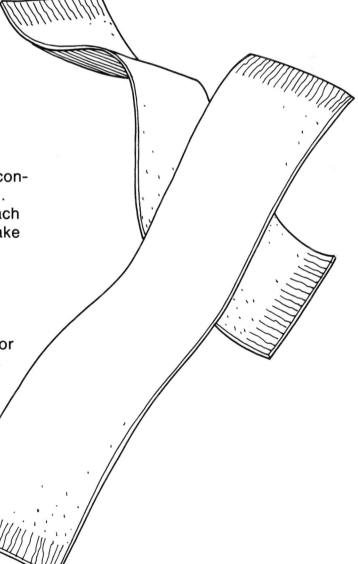

Six Silver Spoons

Just before the beginning of the American Revolution, two children are determined to deliver a special birthday present made by Paul Revere. They want to take six Revere spoons to their mother, and in order to do this they must go through the British lines.

Lowrey, Janette Sebring. New York: Harper and Row, 1971. 64 pages, illustrated, preschool–grade 2

 ACTIVITY: Learn about a famous American, Paul Revere.

Materials

Six silver spoons (or other silver items)

A copy of Longfellow's poem "Paul Revere's Ride" (optional)

Procedure

Give a brief history of the importance of Paul Revere before and during the American Revolution. Tell students that he was a master silversmith who also made surgical instruments, sold spectacles, replaced missing teeth, and engraved copper plates. Students might enjoy hearing you read Longfellow's narrative poem "Paul Revere's Ride," which commemorates his ride on April 18, 1775, to warn that the redcoats were on their way.

Before you read the story, show the silver spoons to the students. Explain that Paul Revere made spoons and other items out of silver.

The Supermarket

A mother and her son go to the supermarket to buy groceries. "I like the way the door opens all by itself," the boy thinks. He helps do all the shopping, but when they get home, he notices that they forgot something.

Rockwell, Anne, and Harlow Rockwell. New York: Macmillan, 1979.

24 pages, illustrated, preschool–grade 1

 ACTIVITY: Choose merchandise in magazines.

Materials

Old magazines

Scissors

Paste

Construction paper

Note: This activity could be correlated effectively with a unit of study on consumer awareness.

Procedure

Lead students in a discussion of items that can be found at a supermarket. Have students look through magazines and cut out two items that they could find in a supermarket. Have them paste the pictures on a sheet of construction paper.

Allow students to identify their selections and state why they chose each one.

Swimmy

When a family of little red fish is eaten by a large, hungry tuna, Swimmy, a little black fish, is the only survivor. He is sad and lonely. As he explores the ocean, he finds a school of little red fish. Swimmy teaches them how to swim in the formation of a big fish. Swimmy becomes the eye.

Lionni, Leo. New York: Pantheon Books, 1963.
32 pages, illustrated, preschool–grade 2

 ACTIVITY: Make a school of fish.

Materials

White construction paper, large (the number of students will determine the size needed)

Black construction paper, small

Red construction paper, small (for each student)

Black felt-tip pen

Pencils

Scissors

Paste

Thumbtacks or tape

Bulletin board or wall

Procedure

Have each student draw a small fish on red paper and cut it out. While the students are doing this, draw and cut out one small black fish, and draw a large fish on white construction paper.

Have students, in turn, paste their red fish within the outlined area of the big white fish. Paste the black fish in the area where the eye should be. Print the title, "Swimmy," at the top of the paper.

Display the finished work on a bulletin board or a wall.

"There Are Rocks in My Socks!" Said the Ox to the Fox

An ox complains about rocks in his socks. The fox gives him advice, but it's never quite right. The poor ox gets into quite a position by following the fox's advice.

Thomas, Patricia. New York: Lothrop, Lee & Shepard, 1979. 32 pages, illustrated, preschool–grade 3

 ACTIVITY: Use visual aids to share a story.

Materials

Old sock

Rocks

Procedure

Put rocks into the sock. Show the sock to the students and shake it. Allow them to feel the rocks in the sock. Ask the students if they have ever had rocks in their socks. Have them describe what it feels like.

When you are finished reading the story, dump the rocks out of the sock.

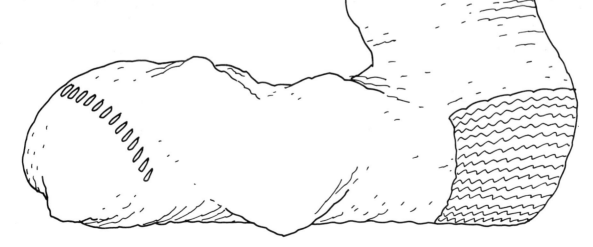

Three Days on a River in a Red Canoe

Two children and their mothers go on a three-day camping trip. They spend a wonderful, adventurous time camping, canoeing, and fishing.

Williams, Vera B. New York: Greenwillow Books, 1981.
32 pages, illustrated, K–grade 3

 ACTIVITY: Draw a picture of yourself in a red canoe.

Materials

Copy of "The Red Canoe," page 47, for each student

Crayons

Procedure

After the story session, distribute copies of "The Red Canoe."

Have each student color the canoe red and then draw a picture of himself or herself in it.

Have each student make up a story about an adventure in a canoe and, in turn, tell it to the other students.

The Red Canoe

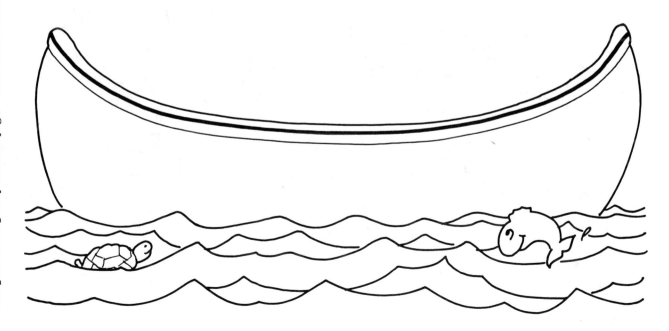

Too Much Noise

An old man who complains about noise in his house seeks
advice from a wise man. The wise man advises him to get various animals that create even more noise.

McGovern, Ann. Boston: Houghton Mifflin, 1967.
48 pages, illustrated, K–grade 3

ACTIVITY: Dramatize a plot.

Materials

Book

Procedure

Encourage students to participate
orally in the story session. Ask them to
make the noises of the characters as
you read the story.

Then select several students to
dramatize the story by playing the parts
of Peter, the leaves, the teakettle, the
bed, the floor, the cow, the donkey, the
sheep, the hen, the dog, the cat, and
the wise man.

Note: Be prepared for a lot of noise.

A Tree Is Nice

What makes a tree nice? Well, all kinds of things. Its leaves, its trunk, its limbs, and the shade that it makes are just some of them. A tree is also a good place to lean your hoe when you rest and a good place to hang a swing from. Trees are nice to plant and nice to watch grow. And a tree is a nice place for a house to be near.

Udry, Janice May. New York: Harper and Row, 1956. 32 pages, illustrated, preschool–grade 1

 ACTIVITY: Discuss uses, values, and products of trees.

Materials

Small branch of a tree, in a container

Nuts

Fruit

Bark

Lumber

Toothpicks

Paper

Note: Arbor Day is a good time to present this activity.

Procedure

Place the container with the tree branch on a table. Place products of trees around it.

Lead students in a discussion about trees. Ask them what they like about trees.

Use the tree products on the table as props while you lead a discussion about some of the products that come from or are made from trees.

Trucks

Detailed illustrations show every kind of truck you can think of:
seven kinds of delivery trucks, four kinds of trucks moving
heavy loads, three kinds of trucks pushing things, five kinds of
trucks pulling things. There are also trucks that lift things,
trucks that dig holes, and more.

Gibbons, Gail. New York: Thomas Y. Crowell, 1981.
32 pages, illustrated, preschool–grade 2

 ACTIVITY: Discuss various kinds of trucks and what they do.

Materials

Toy trucks

Procedure

Have students bring toy trucks to
school on a designated day. (If they
don't have any, they can cut pictures of
trucks out of magazines.)

After reading the story, have students
take turns showing their trucks and
telling something about them. They
can tell what the truck is called and
what it is used for.

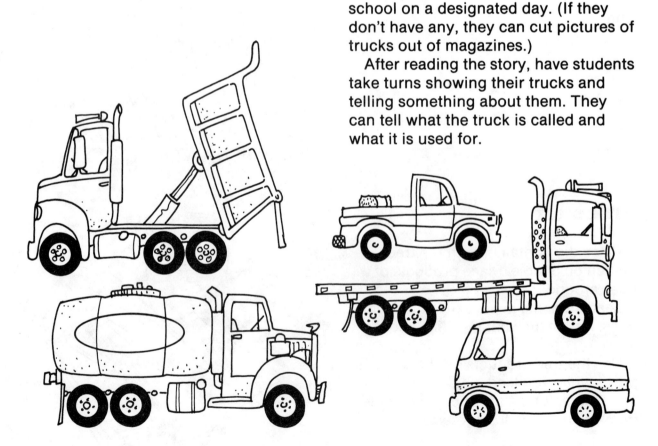

Turtle Tale

A turtle learns that a wise turtle knows when to put its head in its shell and when to stick it out.

Asch, Frank. New York: Dial Press, 1978.

32 pages, illustrated, preschool–grade 2

 ACTIVITY: Answer questions on the worksheet and color the picture of the turtle.

Materials

Copy of "A Wise Turtle," page 52, for each student

Pencils

Crayons

Procedure

Have students check the appropriate responses on the worksheet. Then have them color the picture.

A Wise Turtle

Where should a wise turtle put its head

when it eats?   _____ in its shell   _____ out of its shell

when it sees a fox?   _____ in its shell   _____ out of its shell

when it drinks?   _____ in its shell   _____ out of its shell

when it moves?   _____ in its shell   _____ out of its shell

Color the turtle.

Umbrella

Momo receives an umbrella and red rubber boots on her third birthday and is so excited that she can hardly wait for the rain. On the first rainy day after her birthday, she acts very grown up. She walks straight and doesn't forget her umbrella after nursery school. She even walks without holding her mother's or father's hand.

Yashima, Taro. New York: Viking, 1958.
32 pages, illustrated, preschool–grade 1

 ACTIVITY: Make umbrellas.

Materials

Construction paper

Pencils

Scissors

Procedure

Give each student a sheet of construction paper. Have the children fold their papers in half, widthwise. Have them draw one half of an umbrella, with the middle of the umbrella on the fold. Have them cut their umbrellas out and open them up.

Have the students sit in a circle and take turns in an oral retelling of the story. Have them hold their umbrellas as they retell the story.

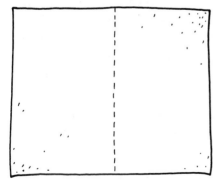 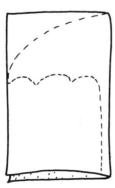 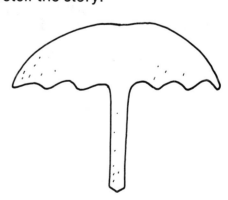

Note: This activity is more fun on a rainy day.

The Very Little Girl
and *The Very Little Boy*

Here are two books by the same author. One is about a very little girl; the other is about a very little boy. They are smaller than all the things around them. They are so small that they can't do many of the things they want to do. But something happens: they grow!

Krasilovsky, Phyllis. *The Very Little Girl.* New York: Doubleday, 1953.
36 pages, illustrated, K–grade 1
———. *The Very Little Boy.* New York: Doubleday, 1962.
36 pages, illustrated, K–grade 1

 ACTIVITY: Measure the students' heights.

Materials

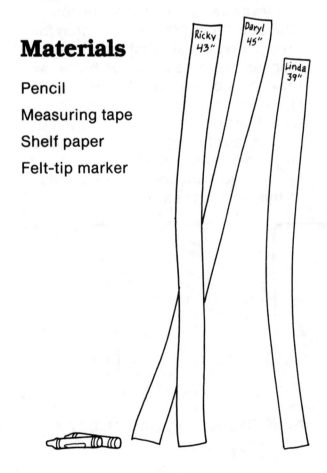

Pencil

Measuring tape

Shelf paper

Felt-tip marker

Procedure

Have the students, in turn, stand straight, back against a wall. Use a pencil to mark a dot on the wall to show how tall each child is. Use the measuring tape to measure from the dot to the floor. Then cut a strip of paper the length of each student's height. With a felt-tip marker, write the student's name, the date, and the student's height on the strip of paper. Save the paper strips, either taped along a wall or stored in a cabinet or closet.

About six months later, repeat this activity. Have the students compare the two strips of paper. Help them determine how much they have grown.

Note: Try to plan this activity early enough in the year to allow for significant growth.

What Mary Jo Shared

Mary Jo wants to share something with her class, but she can't think of anything that hasn't already been shared. She wants to share her new umbrella, but she sees lots of umbrellas in the classroom. She wants to share a grasshopper, but Jimmy brings *six* grasshoppers. Finally, Mary Jo thinks of something. She shares her father.

Udry, Janice May. Chicago: Whitman, 1966.
40 pages, illustrated, K–grade 3

 ACTIVITY: Share something special.

Procedure

In advance, tell students to bring in something to share for a special sharing day. Tell them the date of this special day.

When sharing day arrives, begin the activity by reading the story. Afterward, have the students "show and tell."

When the students have completed their presentations, share something special of your own with them.

What Time Is It, Jeanne-Marie?

Starting at 7:00 in the morning when Jeanne-Marie gets up, we see everything she does during the day. A few French words *(midi, bon appetit, minuit)* and a sentence in French *(La lune rit, bonne nuit)* appear in the story.

Francoise. New York: Charles Scribner's Sons, 1963.
32 pages, illustrated, K–grade 3

 ACTIVITY: Use a clock to show various times of day.

Materials

Clock (any clock, toy or real, on which the hands can be manipulated)

Procedure

Set up the clock so that the entire group can see it. As you read about Jeanne-Marie progressing through the day, change the hands on the clock to correspond to the story.

After you finish reading the story, have students take turns moving the hands of the clock to specific times of day (the time they eat lunch, the time they take a bath, and so on).

A Woggle of Witches

A "woggle" of witches wakes up in the forest on Halloween night. All the witches have some bat stew. Then they circle the moon on their brooms and land in a cornfield, where they are frightened away by some scary trick-or-treaters.

Adams, Adrienne. New York: Charles Scribner's Sons, 1971. 32 pages, illustrated, preschool–grade 1

 ACTIVITY: Make a "woggle" of witches.

Materials

Copy of "A Woggle of Witches Word-Find," page 58, for each student

Construction paper (black, yellow, and other colors)

Pencils

Crayons

Scissors

Paste

Bulletin board

Plastic or cutout paper letters to spell title

Procedure

Distribute construction paper, pencils, crayons, scissors, and glue to the students. Have each of them draw and cut out the shape of a witch from black construction paper. Then have them cut out the shape of a broom from yellow (or another color) construction paper. Have them paste both parts to another sheet of construction paper and use crayons to draw details (such as faces and lines to indicate straw on the broom).

Arrange the finished projects on a bulletin board and add the title, "A Woggle of Witches."

Distribute copies of "A Woggle of Witches Word-Find." Have the students complete the word-find puzzle and the exercise in alphabetizing.

A Woggle of Witches

A Woggle of Witches Word-Find

The words in the box below appear in the story. Find and circle them in the puzzle. The first one is done for you.

bat	witches	run
night	forest	hats
moon	sky	fire
dark	feast	monsters

```
F  P  S  D  A  R  K  F  I  M
O  C  K  S  T  E  W  I  X  Q
R  N  Y  R  U  N  Q  R  J  O
E  L  B  A  T  B  T  E  H  K
S  O  T  L  R  O  H  A  T  S
T  S  W  I  T  C  H  E  S  I
Z  C  X  F  E  A  S  T  C  N
Q  M  O  O  N  M  E  A  S  R
L  C  G  N  I  G  H  T  P  F
M  O  N  S  T  E  R  S  E  W
```

Write the words from the box above in alphabetical order. The first one is done for you.

1. bat _____

2. _____

3. _____

4. _____

5. _____

6. _____

7. _____

8. _____

9. _____

10. _____

11. _____

12. _____

Designed to Delight reproducible page. © 1986 David S. Lake Publishers

The Year at Maple Hill Farm

In January, the bundled-up farmers feed the animals as twilight falls. In February, the goat, the cat, and the pony mothers take care of their babies, and so on through the year. Each of the twelve two-page spreads represents a different month of the year and shows activities associated with that month.

Provensen, Alice, and Martin Provensen. New York: Atheneum, 1978.

32 pages, illustrated, preschool–grade 2

 ACTIVITY: Illustrate a farm scene.

Materials

Drawing paper

Crayons

Bulletin board

Procedure

Distribute drawing paper and crayons to the students. Have each student choose a month and illustrate animal life on a farm during that particular month. Remind students to consider the weather during that month before they begin their drawings.

Display the pictures on a bulletin board.

Yertle the Turtle and Other Stories

When Yertle the Turtle wants a better view of the world, he demands that other turtles pile up in a stack. Yertle perches on top. But poor Mack, at the bottom, has a few problems.

Dr. Seuss. New York: Random House, 1958.

88 pages, illustrated, K–grade 3

 ACTIVITY: Make a stack of turtles.

Materials

Drawing paper

Pencils or crayons

Scissors

Bulletin board

Thumbtacks

Procedure

Have each student draw a turtle, write his or her name on the shell, and cut it out.

Place the students' drawings on the bulletin board, in a stack. Place your own drawing of Yertle on the top.